From;To

Derek Perry

Presentation by *BookLeaf Publishing*

Web: www.bookleafpub.com

E-mail: info@bookleafpub.com

ISBN: 9789357441858

First edition 2023

*Dedicated to the memory of Anderson William
Perry, Jr.*

And Sometimes On

On the island
Under the mountain
And sometimes on
We
Shed off of old restraints
And reacquainted as youths
Ready to greet everything
Like new

Cozy

The 3rd up of 4
On a sleepy side street
A loft
That'd be lonely if it weren't meant
For two
(cozy)
And warm in the mornings
When sunlight stretched through
The Juliet balcony
And all about
The room

In Joke

We found the park but,
never the fountain.
Perhaps,
some funny local thing?
Who knows.
Let's not tell anyone else,
though.

Abeille

Busy as we let ourselves be,
avenues bloomed with opportunity
in passing, pollinated by outside dining tables
and sprayed graffiti script that persuaded,
even though we didn't know the language.

Destinations Lost

Stayed in a doorway
Destinations lost
Now
Travel bound towards each other
Found
In down cast clouds
And a slowly setting sun
Hung in the space
Between arms and waists

Seat by the Water

It was our evening routine
Our seat by the water
And that bend in the bank
Where strayed light behind us
Framed
But didn't light us

And we claimed a bit of night
For our own

Wild and Natural

Away, across the lake
at night,
the lamp light blazed
like a wild and natural thing,
while we sat prey,
captive to the flame
of our own making.

Claimants

Now, we swore by the corner store,
and the route we took to the station,
no longer visitors, but claimants,
as if saying made it so.

And so, we said it,
in broken, supposed French,
eager to believe that this life
could make sense.

We could, at least, pretend.

Our Things

the irony in that
we pack up all our things
in hope that nothings left
of value when we leave

Little Hands

Squirrels follow far too long
Far too comfortable
But cute
And amusing how they plead
Little hands
For little hand outs
Little frowns when we don't feed

We Only

Delighted in their surprise
that we only spoke English,
that seeming to belong,
only took being.

Upon Request

Heated floors

can be yours upon request,
of course.

Only the best

for the freshly made poor.

Marvels of the Vine

Off season,
so the market was small, yet
every stall present
held marvels of the vine
or press
or grindstone, goods
we would never find
at home.

Us, Undeserving

Meats smoked by flame
And cheeses that we didn't know by name
Or by taste

Crafted into platters
Serving up the work of masters
To us undeserving
Havers
Of an app

Folded Wreathes

We arrived
Just in time
To watch the leaves go
From green
To folded wreathes of gold
At our feet

Just Sold

I know.

I know, but

never say never!

This could be home,

if we just sold everything.

Back

I want to be home to you
so that, where ever you go,
you'll know where you belong
and perhaps, you won't be long
back.

Last Train

we sampled sweets
in the Old Town
unexpectedly crowded
so late

found our way out
to the pier
and stayed to watch the stars
til the last train neared.

www.ingramcontent.com/pod-product-compliance
Lightning Source LLC
LaVergne TN
LVHW051252200726
843510LV00011B/1823